T0413989

Pack a Bag

LEVEL 3
/j/y/

DECODABLES BY jump!

Teaching Tips

Yellow Level 3

This book focuses on the phonemes **/j/y/**.

Before Reading

- Discuss the title. Ask readers what they think the book will be about.
- Sound out the words on page 3 together.

Read the Book

- Ask readers to use a finger to follow along with each word as it is read.
- Encourage readers to break down unfamiliar words into units of sound. Then, ask them to string the sounds together to create the words.
- Urge readers to point out when the focused phonics phonemes appear in the text.

After Reading

- Encourage children to reread the book independently or with a friend.
- Ask simple questions about the text to check for understanding. Have them find the pages that have the answers to your questions.

© 2024 Booklife Publishing
This edition is published by arrangement with Booklife Publishing.

North American adaptations © 2024 Jump!
5357 Penn Avenue South
Minneapolis, MN 55419
www.jumplibrary.com

Decodables by Jump! are published by Jump! Library.
All rights reserved. No part of this book may be reproduced in any form without written permission from the publisher.

Library of Congress Cataloging-in-Publication Data is available at www.loc.gov or upon request from the publisher.

ISBN: 979-8-88996-813-9 (hardcover)
ISBN: 979-8-88996-814-6 (paperback)
ISBN: 979-8-88996-815-3 (ebook)

Photo Credits
Images are courtesy of Shutterstock.com. With thanks to Getty Images, Thinkstock Photo and iStockphoto. Cover – Pixel-Shot. 4–5 – Odua Images, Elizaveta Galitckaia. 6–7 – Pixel-Shot. 8–9 – DenisProduction.com, Julia Pleskachevskaia. 10–11 – aabejon, Olga Nikiforova. 14–15 – Shutterstock.

Can you find these words in the book?

jet

yes

yet

you

Can you pack a bag?

Do not jam it in.

It will not all fit in the bag yet.

Will it shut if he gets rid of the hat?

Do you need a jet? No. Do not pack it.

Sit on the bag. Will it shut?

Jab and tuck it all in. Will it fit yet?

Yes, it can all fit. You can pack a bag.

Can you say these sounds and draw them with your finger?

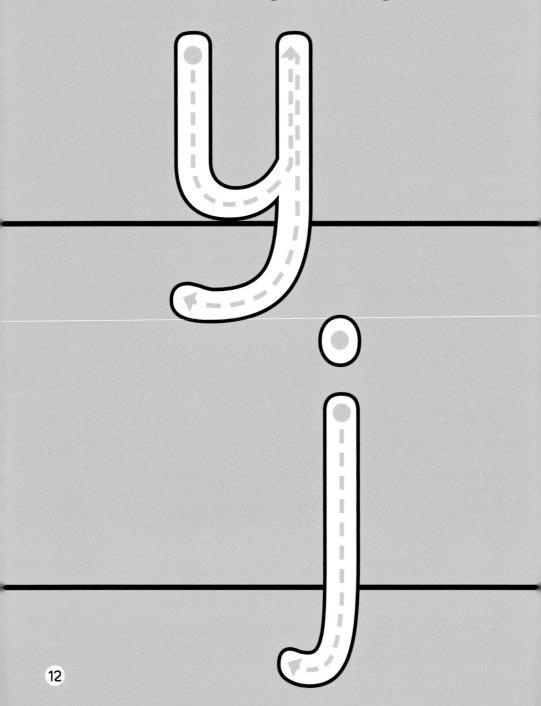

Trace the missing letter to finish each word. Say the words out loud.

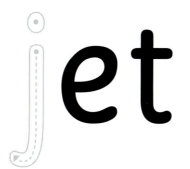 jet

 yes

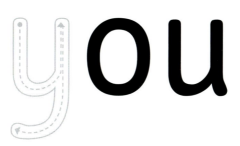 you

What other words can you spell with /y/?

__arn

__ak

__ogurt

What other words can you spell with /j/?

__am

__ar

__eans

Practice reading the book again:

Can you pack a bag?
Do not jam it in.
It will not all fit in the bag yet.
Will it shut if he gets rid of the hat?
Do you need a jet? No. Do not pack it.
Sit on the bag. Will it shut?
Jab and tuck it all in. Will it fit yet?
Yes, it can all fit. You can pack a bag.